Al's Business Cards

by Josh Koenigsberg

A SAMUEL FRENCH ACTING EDITION

SAMUEL FRENCH

FOUNDED 1830

NEW YORK HOLLYWOOD LONDON TORONTO

SAMUELFRENCH.COM

ISBN 978-0-573-69918-4   Printed in U.S.A.   #29811

MUSIC USE NOTE

Licensees are solely responsible for obtaining formal written permission from copyright owners to use copyrighted music in the performance of this play and are strongly cautioned to do so. If no such permission is obtained by the licensee, then the licensee must use only original music that the licensee owns and controls. Licensees are solely responsible and liable for all music clearances and shall indemnify the copyright owners of the play and their licensing agent, Samuel French, Inc., against any costs, expenses, losses and liabilities arising from the use of music by licensees.

IMPORTANT BILLING AND CREDIT
REQUIREMENTS

All producers of *AL'S BUSINESS CARDS must* give credit to the Author of the Play in all programs distributed in connection with performances of the Play, and in all instances in which the title of the Play appears for the purposes of advertising, publicizing or otherwise exploiting the Play and/ or a production. The name of the Author *must* appear on a separate line on which no other name appears, immediately following the title and *must* appear in size of type not less than fifty percent of the size of the title type.

AL'S BUSINESS CARDS was first produced by AT PLAY (Harrison David Rivers, Artistic Director; Kelcie Beene and Carly Hugo, Producers) in association with OLD VIC: NEW VOICES (Kevin Spacey, Artistic Director; Rachael Stevens, New Voices Network Manager) at Theatre Row in New York City in August, 2009. It was directed by Lauren Keating; the set design was by Jian Jung and Tsubasa Kamei; the costume design was by Melissa Trn; the lighting design was by Tito Fleetwood Ladd; the sound design was by Amy Altadonna; and the production stage manager was Amanda Kate Joshi. The cast was as follows:

AL GURVIS	Azhar Khan
EILEEN LEE	Lauren Hines
BARRY BARRINI	Bobby Moreno
DANIEL LUCE	Malcolm Madera
JOSE ALVAREZ	Gabriel Gutierrez

CHARACTERS

AL GURVIS – A gaffing assistant. Light-skinned Indian male who almost looks Hispanic. Has aspirations.

BARRY BARRINI – Al's co-worker. White male. Not the brightest bulb.

EILEEN LEE – A real-estate agent. White female. Recovering alcoholic.

DANIEL LUCE – Eileen's soon-to-be-ex-husband. White male. Alcoholic.

JOSE ALVAREZ – Private Investigator. Hispanic male. Slick.

SETTING

Elizabeth, New Jersey

TIME

Friday afternoon through Monday morning

For Azhar.

Scene One

*(Friday afternoon. Two gaffing assistants, **BARRY**, who's white, and **AL**, a light-skinned Indian who almost looks Hispanic, stand by a craft service table on a film set in Jersey. **BARRY** munches from a bag of chips, **AL** makes himself a coffee and sips it.)*

AL. Hey, I tell you I got business cards.

BARRY. Who did.

AL. Me – I did.

BARRY. *(chuckling)* What? What for?

AL. What do you mean, "what for"?

BARRY. I mean what the hell you need business cards for?

AL. 'Cause I'm in a business, Barry. I'm looking for greater opportunities in the business that I'm in, so I made myself business cards, what's the problem?

*(**BARRY** giggles, shakes his head and munches. **AL** sips his coffee.)*

Yo, I tell you what happened though?

BARRY. *(mockingly)* What, with your *business cards?*

AL. Yeah, with my fucking business cards.

BARRY. *(laughing)* What do these business cards say on 'em anyways?

AL. What do you mean, "What do they say on 'em?" They say, "Al Gurvis, Professional Gaffing Assistant."

*(**BARRY** bursts out laughing.)*

Honest to God, what's your problem?

BARRY. What'd you hire a secretary also?

AL. *(shaking his head)* You're a fuck-stick.

7

BARRY. Hey, what extension do I dial to get you? Can I borrow the company car? Hey, how were the profit margins this quarter? *(chuckles)* Business cards…

AL. Yeah, that's right, business cards! Y'know some people want to advance in the world, not stand around scratching their butt all day, munching loudly on chips or whatever.

(**BARRY** *eats a chip loudly.* **AL** *slurps his coffee indignantly.*)

I tell you what happened with them though?

BARRY. No, Al – what happened with your business cards.

AL. Alright, so I order 'em from ABC Printers, right? – supposedly the best fucking print shop in Jersey – and I get a call last Monday saying they're ready. Fine. I go in, pick 'em up, take 'em home. Know what they say on 'em?

BARRY. No, what do they say on 'em?

AL. They say, "Eileen Lee – Executive Realtor."

(**AL** *looks at* **BARRY** *expectantly.* **BARRY** *munches. They stare at each other.*)

They say, "Eileen Lee – Executive Realtor."

BARRY. I heard you – who's Eileen Lee.

AL. Not fucking me, that's who. See what happened is they must've mixed up my cards with hers. So I call her up.

BARRY. Wait a minute, you know her?

AL. What? No, fucktard, her number's on the fucking business cards.

BARRY. Oh right, okay.

AL. So I call her up, I go, "Is this Eileen Lee, Executive Realtor?" She goes, "Yeah, who's this." I go, "It's Al Gurvis, I got your business cards." She goes, "Great, I'll be in to pick 'em up this week." I go, "Nah nah, it's not the printers calling honey. It's *me*, Al Gurvis. I got your business cards."

BARRY. *(chuckling)* What do you, gotta spell it out for her?

AL. I know, right? She's like, "Wait a minute – *Al Gurvis* – where do I know that name from. Are you in the program?"

BARRY. "*Program*" – what program?

AL. Oh, that's what they call A.A., I think.

BARRY. Jesus, she's an alcoholic to boot?

AL. What do you mean, "to boot?" Nah, she's in recovery or whatever.

BARRY. Aw, that's a myth.

AL. Huh?

BARRY. "Recovery." You are who you are – once an alcoholic, always an alcoholic.

AL. Well, that's your opinion.

BARRY. What, you don't agree?

AL. The point is I'm like, "No, you don't know me from the fucking program. You know me cause you got my business cards and I got yours."

BARRY. What, she didn't notice?

AL. No, she's like, "I *do*?" I'm like, "*Yes*, you do. *That's* how come you know my name, honey." So she checks, sure enough she finds 'em. She goes, "Ohhh, that's right! So *you're* Al Gurvis." I go, "Yes, I'm Al Gurvis – Professional Gaffing Assistant."

BARRY. *(chuckling)* Why the fuck did you write "Professional Gaffing Assistant?" Why not just call yourself, "Electrician." They're practically the same thing.

AL. 'Cause I'm not an electrician, I'm a professional gaffing assistant.

BARRY. Yeah, but no one's gonna know what that is. I don't even think that's a real title.

AL. No, but y'know – they'll probably go, "Professional gaffing assistant – what's that? Oh, it's probably like an electrician. I know – I'll hire him to do electrical work."

BARRY. Who the fuck is gonna say that?

AL. Y'know – people. People are smart.

BARRY. If they're so smart, they'll know the difference between a licensed electrician and "Professional Gaffing Assistant." Just say "Electrician."

AL. Nah, I'm not gonna lie.

BARRY. Well, Jesus, Al, you're misleading them as it is.

AL. What do you mean I'm misleading them as it is?

BARRY. C'mon, Al. *(beat)* Y'know.

AL. No, I don't know – what are you talking about?

BARRY. What, I gotta say it?

AL. Say what?

BARRY. Jesus Christ. Look, even if they're idiots, and they say, "Oh he's not a licensed electrician, he's close enough, we'll hire him anyways" – don't you think they're gonna feel a *little* misled when they hire "Al Gurvis" and *you* show up?

AL. Why wouldn't I show up. I'm Al Gurvis.

BARRY. I know you're Al Gurvis. But Christ, Al – they think they're hiring a white electrician and instead they get this lying Hispanic? You're credibility's gonna go to shit.

(**AL** *slurps his coffee.*)

Nah, I mean I'm not saying…I mean, look, it could be worse. It's not like you're from the middle-east or something. Some *towel-head*. Nah, I'm just saying, as long as you're a Hispanic guy with an American guy's name, you might as well call yourself an "Electrician."

(**BARRY** *grabs a can of soda and opens it. They stare at each other.*)

AL. First off? I'm Indian.

BARRY. Who's Indian.

AL. Me. I'm Indian.

BARRY. Who *you*? You're not Indian.

AL. Uh, yes, actually. Yes, I am.

(**BARRY** *looks him over.*)

BARRY. Nah.

AL. No, I'm not asking you. I'm telling you – I'm Indian. I'm half-Indian.

BARRY. Half-Indian, half-Hispanic?

AL. No, just half-Indian.

BARRY. And the other half – what, half-American?

AL. *(annoyed)* Well, I'd like to think I'm *all* American.

BARRY. Well, not technically.

AL. Look, my mom grew up in India! My dad's, I don't know, some kind of Irish. But I grew up here, I don't have a fucking accent.

BARRY. No, I know – I didn't say that. I know your deal. I just thought your mom was from Mexico or whatever.

AL. Well, she's not, she's from India, so what's your point?

BARRY. Huh? No, I don't have a *point*, I'm just saying. Y'know – be careful. Cause the world's a fucked up place, y'know? No, I did not know that you were from India or whatever.

*(**BARRY** munches awkwardly.)*

Man, I'm tired, I got like no sleep last night. *(offering the bag)* Hey, you want some?

AL. No, I don't wanna touch 'em with my lying Hispanic hands.

BARRY. Aw, c'mon. Besides you said you weren't Hispanic.

AL. Oh – so what, if I was, you wouldn't give me none?

BARRY. What? No! But y'know it's a moot point, or whatever. I mean Indian's good. Indian's better.

AL. Indian's *better*?

BARRY. What? No, c'mon I'm giving you a compliment here.

AL. Oh, you're giving me a *compliment*?

BARRY. Jesus, why's everyone's so sensitive these days! We're just talking here.

AL. All right, let me ask you a question, Barry. Let's say someone gets my business card.

BARRY. *(trying to lighten the mood)* Yeah, after you get 'em back from that alcoholic, am I right?

*(**BARRY** smiles. **AL** doesn't.)*

AL. Let's say someone gets my card...

BARRY. Uh huh...

AL. Wants to hire me...

BARRY. *Very* possible...

AL. Then I show up. Are they gonna be pissed that I'm a lying Indian?

BARRY. No!

*(**AL** nods and walks away.)*

But y'know, cause you'll tell them.

*(**AL** stops and turns back.)*

AL. What'll I tell them?

BARRY. Y'know. That you're only *half* or whatever. I mean I think we're in agreement here.

AL. No, we're not in agreement.

BARRY. *(snaps his fingers)* I got it: you put your picture on the business card.

AL. My what? My *picture?*

BARRY. Yeah, you get 'em back from this Real Estate Drunk and then you redo 'em. You put your picture on the card. That way, if someone wants to hire you, they'll know what they're getting themselves into.

AL. Y'know what? Fuck you.

BARRY. Fuck me? What for?

AL. Cause you're an idiot! If someone gets my card, wants to hire me, they're not gonna give a shit what I look like! If anything, it's a, it's a...*pleasant surprise!*

BARRY. Hey look, Al, I'm with you. *(beat)* But it's just not true.

AL. Oh really? So what – you think when I go to pick up the cards from this Eileen Lee, she's gonna see me, scream, and run in the other direction?

BARRY. What, you're gonna go see her? Today?

AL. Yeah, after work or whatever. I made a 'date' or whatever to pick 'em up.

BARRY. "*A date*"? *(looks at him curiously)* When was the last time you got laid?

AL. What? Fuck you. I gotta use the bathroom.

BARRY. Okay, how about this: let's make a wager.

AL. A what? No.

BARRY. Aw, c'mon, this is perfect! You're gonna go see Eileen Lee – okay. She'll be our guinea pig. If she doesn't say anything about how your name and face don't match – you win.

AL. What'll I win?

BARRY. You win, uh…I don't know, a box of fucking chocolates.

*(**AL** starts walking away.)*

Ghirardelli Chocolates.

AL. *(He loves those.)* All right, fine. Now I gotta use the bathroom before break's up.

BARRY. Whoa, whoa, whoa. What if you lose.

AL. I won't. She's not gonna say anything.

BARRY. Yeah, but what if she does.

AL. Jesus Christ, Barry, I don't know. I'll get *you* a box of chocolates.

BARRY. I don't like chocolates.

AL. Well what *do* you like?

BARRY. Scotch.

AL. Fine. It's a little expensive, but okay, I'll buy you a bottle of cheap Scotch. But trust me, she's not gonna say anything.

BARRY. What makes you so sure?

AL. 'Cause that's my whole point – you got a pessimistic outlook on life and people don't work that way! Besides, we're talking about a nice polite Asian girl here.

BARRY. Asian? What did she, have an accent on the phone?

AL. What? No, but c'mon – Eileen *Lee?*

BARRY. Whatever. It's a deal though, right?

AL. Yeah, okay, it's a deal.

(**BARRY** *wipes his Frito hand on his pants and offers it to* **AL**. **AL** *shakes on it.* **BARRY** *pulls him in close.*)

BARRY. Remember, we're using the honor system here. Don't go lying to me and telling me on Monday that she didn't say nothing if she did. I'll be able to see it on your face.

(*The buzzer rings signaling the end of the break.*)

AL. Aw, great. Alright, I gotta use the bathroom.

BARRY. That's three times you told me. What do you, want me to wipe your ass for you?

End of Scene

Scene Two

(Friday afternoon, later. **AL** *sits at a Starbucks, drinking a coffee. A box of business cards sits on the table in front of him. His leg shakes from all the caffeine. He looks around for* **EILEEN LEE**. *From behind him,* **EILEEN LEE** *walks in, dressed in a well-fitting suit. She is not Asian. She looks around and sees the box on Al's table. She approaches him tentatively.)*

EILEEN. Al Gurvis?

AL. *(turns to look at her)* Yeah.

EILEEN. *(extending a hand)* Hi. Eileen Lee.

AL. Really?

EILEEN. Really. *(smiling)* Let me guess – you thought I'd be Asian.

AL. Who me? No, no. *(beat)* Why – you get that a lot?

EILEEN. Um, from time to time. It's the name I guess. Although I don't really get the connection. I mean the general of the confederate army was named Robert E. *Lee*, so. Who knows?

(She shrugs and smiles politely. **AL** *nods, staring at her. He's very attracted to her.)*

Sorry to sneak up on you like that by the way.

AL. Yeah, I was gonna say, I was looking for you over by, uh…by here. So were you in the bathroom this whole time?

EILEEN. Uh, no, I just came in. There's another door, right there.

AL. *(seeing it)* Oh, no kidding. Hey, to think, I could've come in that way.

*(***AL*** *smiles like he's just made a joke.)*

EILEEN. Yup. That's another way to come in.

AL. Yeah. So you want a coffee or something?

EILEEN. Oh. I, uh, I would, but I was just sort of on my way home. Well, I was heading to a meeting first, and *then* I was going home, but anyway. Y'know it's funny actually – I expected you to look a little different too.

AL. *(sensing disaster)* What, you mean like cause of my voice on the phone, you thought I'd be younger or something.

EILEEN. No, actually I expected you be, uh, well…white.

(**EILEEN** *shrugs and chuckles.* **AL** *nods, upset that he's lost the bet.*)

Sorry – was that inappropriate to say?

AL. Nah, nah. *(disappointed)* Y'know, it's just the world we live in, right?

EILEEN. No, but I was going to say, if anything, I'm glad I was wrong. I mean if anything, it's a…a pleasant surprise, y'know?

AL. *(excited)* It *is*, right! I mean you don't want to see another boring white guy walking around Jersey, right?

EILEEN. *(agreeing)* Oh no – definitely not! I mean you're, what – Indian? Half-Indian?

AL. Half-Indian, that's right!

EILEEN. Yeah, that's much more interesting. And what's the other half?

AL. Oh, uh, some kind of Irish, I don't know. I didn't really know my dad that well.

EILEEN. Oh. Well, who cares, right?

AL. Yes, exactly – who cares! The important thing is that it was a *pleasant surprise*, am I right? *(to himself)* No, I think I won this bet.

EILEEN. Hmm? What bet?

AL. Oh no – it was just this little thing. Me and my buddy, y'know.

EILEEN. You and your buddy?

AL. Yeah, he's a *(makes a jerking-off motion)*. He thought when you saw me you'd be like horrified or something.

EILEEN. That I'd be horrified?

AL. Or y'know – 'freaked out' or whatever. That my name and face don't match.

EILEEN. Well, your friend obviously doesn't have a very positive or mature outlook on life.

(**AL** *is so excited, he tries to say three things at once.*)

AL. Ye – Exa – Okay, now I *have* to buy you a cup of coffee.

EILEEN. Oh no, really that's okay.

AL. Listen, take it to go if you want. Take it to your meeting or what have you. But I am buying you this cup of coffee. How do you like it?

EILEEN. Um, well, with half-and-half and sugar, but –

AL. Okay – small, medium, or large?

EILEEN. Um, I usually get a grande, but –

AL. One grande coffee coming right up.

(**AL** *exits towards the side where* **EILEEN** *came in.* **EILEEN** *stands there. She sees the box on the table. She goes to open it.*)

(*re-entering*) They ran out of grande cups. You want a small or a large?

EILEEN. Oh, uh, I'll just take a tall then.

AL. *(beat)* That's a small, right?

EILEEN. Yes, right.

(**AL** *nods and exits.* **EILEEN** *watches him go. She opens the box and checks the cards inside, making sure they look right. She closes it up again.* **AL** *re-enters with a cup.*)

AL. And here is one tall coffee on me.

EILEEN. Well, thank you very much, Al.

AL. Listen, it's the least I could do considering you just won me a box of my favorite chocolates – Ghirardelli Chocolates. You ever have those? They sell 'em at that place 'Vintage Chocolates' on Atalanta Plaza. You ever been there?

EILEEN. No, I don't think so.

AL. Oh, it's great, you gotta check it out – just past the Turnpike. It's like two minutes from my place on Livingston and New Point. But y'know, I don't go that often cause of, y'know –

(AL pats his stomach, signaling that he doesn't want to get too fat. EILEEN smiles and nods. She points to the box.)

EILEEN. So are those the, uh…?

AL. Huh? Oh yeah, I got your cards right here. *(chuckling)* We got so carried away, I almost forgot. Here.

(He hands the box to her. She takes them.)

EILEEN. Great. Thanks.

(She opens them up and looks at them.)

Oh, they look great. Y'know, they really *do* do a good job over there.

AL. Oh at ABC? Yeah, best print shop in Jersey, you ask me.

EILEEN. Definitely. Well anyway, thanks so much, Al. It was great meeting you.

AL. Yeah, you too.

EILEEN. *(getting up)* And, uh, good luck with everything.

AL. Yeah, same. *(making a joke)* Hey, good luck with the name!

(EILEEN starts to leave.)

EILEEN. *(smiling)* Thanks.

AL. Yeah. *(suddenly realizing)* Hey hold up – Eileen.

EILEEN. Hmmm?

AL. You got mine too, right?

EILEEN. Your…?

AL. Y'know, my business cards.

EILEEN. Oh. Uh, no, I dropped them off at the printers.

AL. What, at ABC?

EILEEN. Yeah. Oh my God, I thought – I thought I told you on the phone. I dropped them off right after you called last Monday, so you could pick them up if you needed them.

AL. Oh. Well, so you couldn't've told me on the phone. Y'know, if you did it *after* we spoke.

EILEEN. *(embarrassed)* Right. God, I'm such an idiot. I'm so sorry.

AL. *(trying not to be mad)* Nah, nah. That's, uh, that's okay. Uh. Let me just call 'em up, I'm sure they have 'em.

(**AL** *takes out his cell phone.*)

EILEEN. Okay. God, I'm so sorry. In hindsight, it seems really dumb.

AL. *(dialing)* Yup.

(**AL** *listens to the phone ring. And ring.*)

Aw great, they're fucking closed!

EILEEN. *(a little shocked from his obscenity)* Oh. Uh, gee.

AL. Y'know, it's just that they're closed for the whole fucking weekend now.

EILEEN. Oh my God, really?

AL. Yeah, they close for the weekends there – bunch of fucking amateurs!

(**AL** *notices his language has upset* **EILEEN**.*)

Oh. Uh, sorry, I don't mean to curse so much.

EILEEN. No, I understand. I mean who closes their business on the weekends, right?

AL. A bunch of fucking amateurs, that's who! Aw, crap, there I go again. Sorry.

EILEEN. No, that's fine.

AL. Hey you don't know offhand if they looked okay? My business cards, I mean.

EILEEN. Oh. Uh, I think they were fine. I mean I took one out when you called, just to check the name on it. I don't think I noticed anything wrong.

AL. So it said "Al Gurvis" and it spelled it G-U-R-V-I-S.

EILEEN. Yup, I think so. It said, "Al Gurvis – Professional Gassing Assistant."

AL. Wait a minute – it said *what?*

EILEEN. Uh, it said "Al Gurvis – Professional Gassing Assistant."

AL. Aw, f – *(He stops himself from cursing. He composes himself.)* It's 'Professional *Gaffing* Assistant. Not, uh, not 'Gassing.' '*Gassing*?!'

EILEEN. *(chuckling)* Oh my God, you're kidding. They didn't send you a proof?

AL. Nope. Nope!

EILEEN. And they're usually so good there. I guess the 'F's must've looked like 'S's?

AL. Yeah well. *(beat)* Anyway, it's not your problem, right?

(AL sighs and sits down. EILEEN watches him, guiltily, not knowing what to do. She goes back to the table.)

EILEEN. Tell you what, let me – let me buy *you* a cup of coffee.

AL. Huh? Oh no – that's all right. I got one already. Besides, it's not your fault.

EILEEN. Well, one – it sort of is. And two – I should at least repay the favor. Tell you what – I'll get you a pastry instead, how's that?

AL. A pastry? What, like one of those Banana ones there?

EILEEN. Yeah, I'll get you a Banana one. It's the least I can do for screwing this up.

(AL shrugs, clearly wanting one. EILEEN puts her box down and goes to get a pastry. AL waits until she's out of sight, then opens the box of cards and pockets one. He smells himself and fixes his hair. EILEEN comes back with a pastry.)

So just out of curiosity, what *is* a Professional Gaffing Assistant anyway?

AL. Oh, it's sort of like an Electrician. You help out with electrical work on film and TV sets.

(**AL** *takes a huge bite of the pastry.*)

EILEEN. Oh, that's so cool. So do you, like, work with a bunch celebrities and stuff?

AL. *(with his mouthful.)* No, not really.

(**EILEEN** *nods, disappointed.*)

AL. Well, sometimes. Sometimes! Actually, you know who's on the set that I'm working on now is, uh, what's his face – John Stamos.

EILEEN. No!

AL. Yeah, we talked about the weather the other day. And uh, Robin Tunney – you know her?

EILEEN. Sure! She was in that horror movie a while back! Oh my God, so what movie is it?

AL. Uh, it's called "Killing Mr. Kissel." Or "The Two Mr. Kissels"? Y'know it's for Lifetime.

EILEEN. Oh, okay. So you work for Lifetime.

AL. Who, me? Nah. I mostly do freelance stuff.

EILEEN. Ah, I see. And is it steady work?

AL. Steady enough that I got a shitty one bedroom that smells like cat piss.

EILEEN. Oh I love cats, how many do you have?

AL. Who me? Nah, I don't got any, I'm allergic.

EILEEN. Oh.

AL. Oh, no, but my place is on Livingston and New Point, so, y'know – it stinks.

EILEEN. Uh huh. Well *(She clears her throat.)* I mean, I hope you don't mind me asking, but how much do you pull down after taxes?

AL. Who me? I don't know, about thirty. Thirty-five.

EILEEN. Wait, and you're living on Livingston and New Point?

AL. Yeah, why – I could do better?

EILEEN. You're kidding right?

(**AL** *shakes his head, shrugs.* **EILEEN** *opens up her business card box and takes one out. She takes out a pen and writes on the back.*)

EILEEN. *(writing)* Oh my God, this is so perfect. This is like fate or something. You know I do this for a living right? Listen, Al – if you're making 30 to 35 a year, the idea that you're living at Livingston and New Point is laughable. I mean you're practically *on* the turnpike!

AL. It *is* sort of a shit-hole. And y'know I'm trying to branch out and do electrical work too – so that would be like an extra five G's a year. Ten if I'm lucky.

EILEEN. *(hands him the card)* Well what do you think about Westminster Ave.

AL. *Westminster Ave??* You're fucking kidding, right?

EILEEN. That's the thing Al – I'm *not* fucking kidding.

(**AL** *smiles at her vulgarity.*)

EILEEN. *(pointing to the card)* Look, come meet me at this address on Sunday morning – they're having an Open House. First of all, it's this beautiful 2 bedroom, 2 bathroom. Backyard, patio, the works. And second of all, the sellers are in a rush to turn it so it's going way less than market value. Now obviously I can't guarantee anything, but trust me, for a guy making 30 to 35 a year, it shouldn't be a problem.

AL. You serious? Cause I tell you – if there's one place that don't smell like cat piss, it's Westminster Ave.

EILEEN. *(chuckling)* It's true. And not only that. But we'd be neighbors.

(**AL** *stares at her, thinking about the possibilities. End of scene.*)

Scene Three

(Friday night. The small kitchen of a modest house. Something drops loudly from another room. **DANIEL,** *wearing a business suit and a ski mask, lugs a TV set into the kitchen. He puts it down to catch his breath. He takes out a flask and swigs. He looks around the room, as if recalling memories of happier times, and takes another swig.* **EILEEN** *enters from the back door and throws her keys into a dish.* **DANIEL** *turns around suddenly at the sound. They stare at each other.)*

DANIEL. Oh what? You got something to say to me? Thinking of some witty zinger to throw my way? Well, look at you – aren't you so smart. Aren't you so great with your little organized life, throwing your little organized keys, into your happy little key dish. What great little nooks and crannies you've decorated this place with! *(grabbing things)* Oh look, here's a nook! Here's a nook! Look, a house full of nooks, a house full of nooks! Well, nook it up, baby! That's right, that's what I say. Go on. Cover your whole little wonderful happy life with more happy little nooks! That'll make it all more palatable, more agreeable. Yes, let's all just agree, we don't want any conflict! Oh no – we don't like any yelling and screaming! And for your information, yes I have been drinking again, and no, it doesn't interfere with my life. Maybe the weaker willed of us can't handle it, but I can. I'm strong! *(He goes to the TV and lifts it.)* See! I'm strong and I'm on top of things for your information, and in case you're wondering my new apartment is nicer than you're house! Hear what I said? *Your* house, it's *your* house. I don't care. I'm happy. Enjoy *your* house. Go on, buy some more nooks for *your* house! See if *that* helps!

EILEEN. Why are you wearing a ski-mask.

DANIEL. 'Cause the fall air dries out my skin!

(They stare at each other. **DANIEL** *takes off the ski-mask.)*

DANIEL. *(cont.)* And I didn't want our neighbors to see me. Oh excuse me – *your* neighbors. They're *your* neighbors now. No that's okay, that's fine.

EILEEN. Daniel.

DANIEL. What.

EILEEN. Give me the keys.

DANIEL. For your information, I don't have the keys! I gave 'em back to you weeks ago, remember?! No, what happened is you stupidly left the door unlocked! I guess you don't care if *your* house is now open to the public.

EILEEN. Daniel.

DANIEL. What?! Stop saying my name like that!

EILEEN. Give me the keys.

(DANIEL sighs. He reaches into his pocket and takes out a set of keys. He places them in the key dish in an overly gentle way.)

DANIEL. *(in a baby voice)* There you go wittle key dish. There you go.

(DANIEL walks back to the TV set.)

Now, if you'll excuse me, I have to get home to my new apartment so I can watch the last episode of *Planet Earth* – or as I like to call it – 'What Used To Be Our Favorite Show!'

(DANIEL picks up the TV set.)

EILEEN. Put it down or I'm calling the cops.

DANIEL. *(imitating her)* "*Put it down or I'm calling the cops.*"

EILEEN. Daniel.

DANIEL. *Eileen. Eileen.*

(EILEEN glares at him. He puts the TV down and takes another swig from his flask.)

EILEEN. All right – one: I should call the cops. But I won't, all right?

DANIEL. Oooo – my lucky day! Maybe I should play the lotto!

EILEEN. Two – you need to get yourself to a meeting. Like *tonight*. There's a nine o'clock on Monroe Ave – I'll drive you. *(beat)* It's right next to Valencia.

(DANIEL suddenly becomes sad.)

DANIEL. Valencia, huh? Our old stomping grounds. *(beat)* You wanna get dinner there afterwards?

EILEEN. If it'll get you to the meeting, then yes, I'll buy you dinner at Valencia afterwards.

DANIEL. I didn't say *buy*, I said *get*! I can still pay for my own dinner thank you very much! I'm still vice-president of sales at Men's Warehouse – which is doing just fine, thank you!

EILEEN. Fine, then you can buy *me* dinner.

DANIEL. Freeloader.

EILEEN. Y'know what? Just get out then!

(She grabs him and pushes him towards the door.)

You wanna drink your life away, go ahead. I don't give a shit what happens to you! Just don't go calling me when you're lying in a ditch somewhere about to die and everyone's wondering what happened to you!

(EILEEN composes herself. DANIEL sighs. He goes over to her.)

DANIEL. *(tenderly)* C'mon – why can't we just be friends?

EILEEN. Y'know, that's what I'm trying to do, and you're making it very difficult.

DANIEL. I know. I know. I'll stop, okay? I'll clean myself up. I promise. I mean we still *care* about each other right? You still think about me from time to time right?

(EILEEN nods.)

DANIEL. I mean we're getting separated – so what?

EILEEN. We're getting divorced.

DANIEL. Look, call it what you want. My point is, it doesn't mean we have to stop caring about each other. Or thinking about each other. Missing each other.

(**DANIEL** *puts his arms around* **EILEEN**'*s waist and goes to kiss her neck.*)

EILEEN. *(pushing him away)* Are you serious?!

DANIEL. What?!

EILEEN. You smell like gin.

DANIEL. I'll shower!

EILEEN. Get the hell out of here!

DANIEL. C'mon, you were asking for it!

EILEEN. Oh please! One – I wasn't asking for it. And two – you *broke* into my house!

DANIEL. Oh, if it isn't Ms. Lists Things In Numerical Order!

EILEEN. All right, get out before I call the cops. Or better yet, before I call my lawyer!

DANIEL. Look at me, I'm Ms. Lister! Ms. Lister-ine! Well I've got a list for you! One – go ahead and call your goddamn lawyer, cause I am taking *everything* in this settlement of ours! And two – I got dirt on you like you wouldn't believe.

EILEEN. That's great. Get out.

DANIEL. Don't believe me?

EILEEN. No.

DANIEL. All right then – let me ask you a question.

EILEEN. No.

DANIEL. Who the fuck is Al Gurvis.

EILEEN. *(beat)* Excuse me?

DANIEL. You heard me. Who the fuck is Al Gurvis.

EILEEN. How the Hell do you even know that name?

DANIEL. You mean how do I know the name of your new little Lover Boy? That's easy. You left his business card by the phone. *(baby voice)* While you were making a wittle date.

EILEEN. He's not my – he's a client, okay?

DANIEL. Oh a *client*? Is that what they're calling it these days?

EILEEN. Okay: one –

> *(EILEEN catches herself listing things and stops. DANIEL looks at her expectantly.)*

He's a client and that's all. In fact, I'm taking him to the Gersten's Open House on Sunday. God, why am I even telling you this?! Just give me back the card.

DANIEL. What card?

EILEEN. Daniel, I'm not in the mood.

DANIEL. What, his business card? I don't fucking have it! I saw it last Monday when I came to pick my shit up.

> *(EILEEN glares at him.)*

I don't!

EILEEN. Oh, like you didn't have my keys!

> *(DANIEL unbuckles his belt and starts pulling down his pants.)*

What the Hell are you doing?

> *(DANIEL pulls down his pants.)*

DANIEL. Strip search me, why don't you. Go ahead! Examine my cavities!

EILEEN. Just empty your pockets.

> *(DANIEL pulls on the sides of his underwear.)*

DANIEL. Here, look – see? I No, Havey.

EILEEN. You're an asshole. I know you're lying.

DANIEL. *(imitating her style of speech)* One – I don't have it. Two – I don't have it. Three –

EILEEN. It better be by the fucking phone.

> *(EILEEN storms out of the room. DANIEL waits for her to go. He lifts the TV and waddles out with it.)*

End of Scene

Scene Four

(Saturday morning. The offices of JOSE ALVAREZ, *a private investigator.* JOSE *sits at his desk in a shirt and tie, on the phone.)*

JOSE. So take it to a repair shop, Ma. What do you mean 'por que'? So you can watch your telenovelas is por que. Nah, I can't go with you Ma, I'm busy. Yeah, I saw the lawyer – he's all bark and no bite. Yeah, he threatened me, but so what? Don't worry what he said. He said: *(reading from his notepad)* "If I persisted to bedevil the multitudes of his reputable patronages he would ceaselessly endeavor to discredit the sanctity of my private investigative license, with the same aplomb which I had employed in my inceptive receipt of it." Yeah, that's right. Well, he knew a lot of sentences like that and he didn't mind using them on me. No sé mama. Porque ese hombre esta loco. No te preocupes yo me puedo cuidar solo.

*(*DANIEL *comes in, hung-over, still in the suit from the last scene. He plops himself down at* JOSE*'s desk.* JOSE *glares at him.)*

Okay, Ma. Yeah, Ma, okay. Look, I gotta go. Porque un borracho de mierda acaba de entrar en mi oficina y puede que tenga que llamar a la policia. So I gotta go. Yeah, I love you too, Ma. Hasta luego.

*(*JOSE *hangs up.)*

DANIEL. What's that, Spanish?

*(*JOSE *looks at* DANIEL *and starts clapping.)*

JOSE. Aw, very good, you're a real fucking genius. *(stops clapping)* Don't you fucking knock?

DANIEL. *(holding his temples)* Can you not do that.

JOSE. What, this?

*(*JOSE *claps louder.* DANIEL *grimaces.)*

DANIEL. Okay, Jesus! I'll knock next time! I just thought we had an appointment is all.

JOSE. When you have an appointment with a Doctor, you just stroll into his office, and take your clothes off? No you sit and you wait to be called in. It's a sign of respect. Especially when you make him see you on a Saturday morning.

DANIEL. Yeah, yeah – what do you got?

(JOSE *takes out a notepad from his back pocket. He opens it up and reads from it.*)

JOSE. Alright, she left the office at quarter to five. Drove straight to the Starbucks on Kapkowski Road, where she talked with this Gurvis guy for about an hour and half.

DANIEL. An hour and half?! What about her meeting?

JOSE. The A.A. meeting? Didn't go to it.

DANIEL. That hypocritical little…no wonder she walked in on me at the house.

JOSE. You mean *her* house?

DANIEL. Oh, whatever. What's he look like?

JOSE. Who Gurvis? He's like a light-skinned Indian version of me.

DANIEL. He's Native American?

JOSE. Huh? No dipshit, *Indian*. As in really Indian. Not everyone's a racist.

DANIEL. Well, what'd they talk about.

JOSE. Well, the high-powered, state-of-the-art microphone I have attached to the end of this notepad recorded everything.

DANIEL. You serious?

JOSE. No, you dumb shit – I have no fucking clue what they talked about. Ask them.

DANIEL. What about the card?

JOSE. You mean the business card you swiped and gave me last Monday?

DANIEL. *(annoyed)* Yeah, yeah – Gurvis' card. You trace it?

JOSE. You mean the business card you swiped and gave me last Monday – which I told you last Monday would cost you five hundred dollars to analyze? Five hundred dollars, which may I remind you, I have yet to see.

DANIEL. I told you I'm good for it.

JOSE. And I think it's good for you, and I'm so happy that the two of you are good for each other.

(DANIEL gets up.)

DANIEL. You know what? I've had enough of your goddamn attitude. I am too hung over to deal with this shit. So either you start treating me, your client, with some respect or I walk.

JOSE. *(waving)* Bye bye.

(DANIEL sighs.)

DANIEL. You at least have an Excedrin?

(JOSE tosses him a vial of Excedrin.)

Water?

JOSE. For clients only. Toilet water's free, though.

DANIEL. All right look – I got *(He pulls out all the money on him.)* three twenties. That's sixty.

JOSE. So you get three twenties worth. Which is what I already told you.

DANIEL. Please, Jose –

JOSE. It's Mr. Alvarez.

DANIEL. Please Mr. Alvarez – I need to know this! How about we strike a deal – you need men's wear, designer jackets, suits tailor-made? I can get 'em for you at the Men's Warehouse – and you're gonna like the way you look, I guarantee it!

JOSE. See, the beautiful thing about five hundred dollars is that it can buy *plenty* of clothes. Or it can buy booze. Or lotto tickets so I can win *more* money.

DANIEL. Okay, so how about this: two suits and I'll give you the three twenties I have now, *plus* the other four thirty I owe you in a month!

JOSE. *(correcting)* Four forty. Four thirty makes four ninety and you owe me five.

DANIEL. Right – plus two suits!

(DANIEL *takes his sports coat off.*)

And a sports coat! Please I have to know! *(beat)* Look, you deal with lawyers right?

JOSE. All the fucking time.

DANIEL. Well her lawyer – he's this guy named Goldberg.

JOSE. A lawyer Goldberg huh?

DANIEL. Yeah, he's a real ball-buster – and he's gonna take me for all I'm worth in this goddamn settlement! But not if I get the dirt on her! I mean do you know how much this hurts already – getting dumped like this? And now, on top of all that, she's stepping out on me? And *I* gotta pay the price for it? That's not right! I mean why me?

JOSE. Look – now you've put *me* in a pickle, Mr. Luce.

DANIEL. Call me Daniel. Please.

JOSE. You've put *me* in a pickle, Mr. Luce. Cause I asked a favor from a friend in forensics. He's a busy guy, he don't play with those tools of his for nothing. He's on a payroll, he could get fired. So I ask him for a favor and he does it for a price. Favors for cash, straight up, ca-ching. So now *I'm* in a pickle.

DANIEL. Here, so you give him this money now – and I'll give you double what I owe in one month, when this is all settled! Just one month! *And* a sports coat!

JOSE. I thought you said two suits.

DANIEL. Plus that! Just please! The card!

(JOSE *sighs. He reaches into his inside pocket and pulls out the business card, which is in a tight plastic seal.*)

JOSE. Tests on fingerprints came back positive on your wife – sorry, *ex*-wife – and positive on you, presumably from when you stole it. Negative on Gurvis.

DANIEL. Negative on Gurvis? How's that possible? *(snaps his fingers)* He must have assistants. I bet the fucker's loaded – a real power player.

JOSE. I doubt it. The guy's an assistant himself. A... *(looks at the card)* ...'Gassing Assistant.'

DANIEL. Oh yeah, what is that?

JOSE. Don't know for sure. I know a Gasser's a term for those old, top-heavy, 1950's muscle cars. So if he's a 'Gassing Assistant' my guess is he works at one of those fancy appointment-only auto showrooms. They got weird names for those specialty jobs.

DANIEL. So what – you think he works at 'Autohaus' on Rahway Ave?

JOSE. Nah, that's a used car dealership. If this guy works on Gassers, it's gotta be at some place more upscale.

DANIEL. Upscale, huh? I knew it – the guy's fucking loaded.

JOSE. There's more though. The card was traced back to ABC Printers on Jefferson.

DANIEL. Well sure – best print shop in Jersey, you ask me.

JOSE. Well, I went down there. Apparently I wasn't the only one asking about your wife.

DANIEL. *Ex*-wife. What do you mean.

JOSE. *(consulting the notebook)* Guy named Barry Barrini. You know him.

(**DANIEL** *shakes his head.*)

Well, according to the clerk, he's got short, black hair, medium build – looks mildly retarded? Anyway, clerk says he came in just before I did yesterday afternoon, right before they closed. Asked if 'Eileen Lee' had been in.

DANIEL. Jesus, how many guys is she sleeping with?! Listen, you gotta find out about this Barry Barrini guy! You gotta track him down and tail him!

JOSE. Well, that would require more money, Mr. Luce. And you already owe me twice what you owed, along with two suits and a sports coat. So I doubt I'll be doing that. But what I will do if you don't pay me is I'll sue. I'll sue your pants off and wear those along with the sports coat. And who knows, maybe I'll just hire this Goldberg guy to represent me. That would teach you a thing or two.

(**DANIEL** *suddenly gets an idea.*)

DANIEL. How about if I throw in a TV set?

(**JOSE** *starts to say no, but then considers it.*)

JOSE. Y'know, my mom *could* use a TV, actually.

End of Scene

Scene Five

(Sunday afternoon. A bar. **BARRY** *stands at a table, watching the Mets game on a bar TV. He holds a beer, which he sips periodically.* **JOSE** *sits in the corner with a beer, reading a paper, looking discreetly at* **BARRY**.*)*

BARRY. *(to the TV set)* C'mon Reyes, run it out. Run it out. *(victoriously)* Boom! There it is! Stolen base number 60.

*(***BARRY*** *looks around to see if anyone else is celebrating. He notices* **JOSE** *looking at him and feels a little self-conscious.)*

(pointing to TV set) Fastest person to 60 steals in a season. Well, fastest Met anyways.

JOSE. He's the best.

BARRY. *(disappointed)* Yeah, he won't break the record though.

*(***JOSE*** *shrugs and nods as if to say 'what can you do?'* **BARRY** *nods and looks at the TV again.* **JOSE** *gets up and goes to* **BARRY**.)*

JOSE. Hey, I don't got my glasses on – what's the score.

BARRY. Four-two – Mets.

JOSE. All right – we might actually win today, huh?

BARRY. Yeah, tell me about it. They've lost five in a row now.

JOSE. It's five in a row they've lost?

BARRY. Five! Count 'em! Three to fucking Cincinnati, two straight to Florida. Last time they won was last Sunday – that's a full fucking week ago!

JOSE. Shi-iiit. They should've beat Cincinnati at least once.

BARRY. Y'know what they do is they beat the good teams, but they lose to the bad ones. Problem is there's more bad teams than good ones, so they lose more than they don't.

JOSE. Makes sense.

BARRY. It ain't cause of Reyes though. That guy can rake.

*(***JOSE*** *nods.)*

Hey, what's Reyes – Hispanic or Black?

JOSE. Who's Reyes? Uh... (**JOSE** *has no idea which one is Reyes.*) ...Hispanic, I think.

BARRY. Yeah but ain't he kind of dark for a Hispanic guy? I mean don't he sort of look black?

(**JOSE** *shrugs, nods.*)

Well, I guess you would know better than me, right?

(**JOSE** *gives* **BARRY** *a look.*)

Nah, I mean...I don't mean, uh... (*He sighs.*) It's just lately I've been unsure about this, y'know? Fucking guy I work with? He's Indian.

JOSE. Oh yeah?

BARRY. Yeah, y'know. No biggie. It's just...I thought he was Hispanic for the longest time.

JOSE. They don't really look alike though.

BARRY. Well, not usually, no. But my buddy – he sort of looks like both.

JOSE. Huh. Well, y'know what I say.

BARRY. No, what.

JOSE. Everyone keeps fucking each other, we're all gonna look the same soon.

(**BARRY** *laughs heartily.*)

BARRY. (*going for a cheers*) Hey, here fucking here! To boning each other!

(*They clink glasses and laugh.*)

JOSE. Yeah. My girlfriend's been driving me nuts, though. You got a girl?

BARRY. Who, me? Nah. Not at the moment. Got laid two Thursdays ago though.

JOSE. Oh yeah? One night stand sort of thing?

BARRY. Y'know.

(**BARRY** *makes a pounding motion and laughs.* **JOSE** *laughs and nods.*)

JOSE. Yeah. Truth be told, I, uh, sort of cheated on my girlfriend a week ago myself.

BARRY. Hey, no kidding.

JOSE. Yeah, you know how it is. *(chuckles)* Got too drunk…

BARRY. *(laughing)* Uh oh!

JOSE. *(laughing)* Yeah it was with this real-estate chick – real hot.

BARRY. Oh yeah? No shit. *(to the TV)* Aw, look at this, they fucking strike out with the bases loaded!

JOSE. Unbelievable. *(beat)* No I was gonna say though – all those real-estate chicks? Man, they're *all* fucking hot.

BARRY. Yeah, tell me about it.

JOSE. Yeah. I mean you seen those chicks who work in Century 21 on Morris Ave?

BARRY. *(nodding as if he has)* Oh fuck yeah – they're hot.

JOSE. Yeah, there's this one who's friends with the girl I slept with. Her name's uh, Ellen? Elizabeth? *(He snaps his fingers.)* Eileen. Eileen Lee.

BARRY. Holy shit – you serious?

JOSE. Yeah, why? You know her?

BARRY. Nah, I never met her before. But I heard of *her*.

JOSE. Oh yeah?

> (**BARRY** *nods. He takes a sip of beer and watches the game. Now* **JOSE** *is really confused.)*

> Nah, it's just…the way you looked up when I said her name, I thought you, like, knew her or something.

BARRY. Who me? Nah. A buddy of mine got involved with her though.

JOSE. Involved, huh? You mean like…*involved?*

BARRY. Yeah, y'know.

JOSE. Yeah, yeah. *(beat)* So he fucked her, huh?

BARRY. *(chuckling)* Who Al? Yeah right, in his dreams. Especially if she's as hot as you say.

JOSE. Oh, so they just like fooled around a little.

BARRY. Huh?

JOSE. No, I mean, did they –

BARRY. *(to the TV)* Come on Ump, that was a fucking strike! *(to* **JOSE***)* Man, Johan can't get any breaks today. Ump's controlling the whole game here!

JOSE. Yeah, yeah.

(**JOSE** *doesn't know what to do. He takes a deep breath, about to try a new tactic.*)

Wait a minute. This friend of yours – Al? You don't mean...well you don't mean Al Gurvis, do you?

BARRY. *(shocked)* Yeah, I do! Holy shit – yeah I do! Wait a minute, you know Al?!

JOSE. Do I know Al?! I can't believe *you* know Al!

BARRY. Of course – you kidding? Wait, so how do you know Al?

JOSE. Who, me and Al? Oh, we go way back.

BARRY. No shit. Hey what'd you say your name was?

JOSE. It's Hector. Hector Gonzalez.

BARRY. Hey Hector – Barry. Barry Barrini. *(They shake hands.)* So what, did you guys like grow up together or something?

JOSE. Uh...

BARRY. Aw, what am I saying? He's *not* Hispanic.

JOSE. Right. No.

BARRY. Right. Sorry. *(chuckling)* No, I was gonna ask if you were staying here illegally, too.

JOSE. Staying here *illegally?*

BARRY. Nah, I mean you're his friend, you know his deal right?

JOSE. Well...I mean it's not his *favorite* topic of conversation.

BARRY. No hey, if I were him, it wouldn't be mine, neither. I mean y'know, he's not a *total* citizen – cause of that stuff with his mom – but, y'know, he ain't an immigrant neither. So.

JOSE. Well, sure, sure. *(beat)* Y'know he's always sort of vague about that stuff with his mom – what exactly was that all about?

BARRY. Oh, he's vague with me, too. From what I gathered it was the usual shit: Dad beat his mom, blah, blah, blah – so she came over here with Al when he was like a kid or something. So y'know he wasn't *technically* born here, doesn't have a green card, but –

JOSE. Right, but he's still one of us.

BARRY. Exactly. Well, he's close enough. The U.S. Government doesn't think so, but whatever. *I'm* not gonna say nothing. So how did you say you know him again?

JOSE. Uh, y'know. We're both into Gassers.

BARRY. Oh cool. *(Beat. They watch the TV.)* Wait, you're both into what?

JOSE. Gassers – y'know top-heavy muscle cars from the 50's?

BARRY. Oh right. *(Beat. They watch the TV.)* Huh. I didn't know Al was into those things.

JOSE. Who Al? Oh yeah, he's obsessed.

BARRY. No shit.

JOSE. Yeah, I guess you gotta be, if you wanna work with them, y'know?

BARRY. Yup. *(Beat. They watch the TV.)* What do you mean – he *works* with them?

JOSE. Well yeah, I mean we work together. That's how I know him.

   *(***BARRY*** *looks at* **JOSE** *confused.)*

BARRY. Wait, what? You work with Al?

JOSE. Yeah, we're both Gassing Assistants.

BARRY. *Gassing Assistants?!*

JOSE. Yeah we work on Gassers together.

BARRY. Like on the weekends?

JOSE. No, full time. *(to the TV)* Hey look strike-three! About time.

   *(***BARRY*** *stares at him.)*

BARRY. I thought you said you couldn't see.

JOSE. Huh? No, it's just a little blurry is all. So how do *you* know Al?

BARRY. We're both gaffers.

JOSE. *Gaffers?* What's a –

(**JOSE** *freezes. He realizes he's made a terrible mistake.*)

BARRY. I'm sorry bro – you said you were a *what?*

JOSE. Huh?

BARRY. Who the fuck are you? You don't work with Al.

JOSE. Huh? No that's not – what the fuck are you talking about, man?

BARRY. And how the fuck do you know about Eileen Lee?

JOSE. Nah, nah, she's just an old – oh hold on one second –

(**JOSE** *takes out his cell phone and pretends to be on a phone call.*)

(into the phone) Hey baby. What, right now? No, I'm watching the game! Okay, Jesus! I'm coming, I'm coming! *(putting his hand over the phone, softly)* Hey I gotta run, but it was great meeting you Barry. Hey look – go Mets!

(**JOSE** *points to the game.* **BARRY** *turns to it as* **JOSE** *runs out.*)

BARRY. Hey, who the fuck are you? Get the fuck back here! Hector!

(**BARRY** *starts walking after him.*)

End of Scene

Scene Six

(Sunday night. Valencia Restaurant. **AL** *is as dressed up as he can be.* **EILEEN** *is in a dress. They're at a very small table, where the seats are extremely close to each other.* **AL** *has wine,* **EILEEN** *has water. They're laughing.)*

AL. *(laughing)* No, he freaking did! He sounded *exactly* like Christopher Walken!

EILEEN. *(laughing)* He did not!

AL. *(in a bad Christopher Walken voice)* "And this here – is the master bathroom – where even my dog – comes to lay his poops. Not outside. But in here. He's a trained – pooch."

EILEEN. *(laughing)* Okay – that *is* what he said, but he sounded nothing like Christopher Walken. And neither do you for that matter.

AL. Aw, whatever. You see that freaking patio though? Je-sus!

EILEEN. Listen, I've seen a lot of patios in my day. I can say with confidence, that that's the nicest patio I ever seen.

AL. Comes with a grill and everything! And be careful, cause I can see your place from it.

EILEEN. What are you implying – you're gonna spy on me?

AL. No, hey listen. I'm just saying, sometimes – I like to sunbathe in the nude.

EILEEN. Oh really?

AL. Yeah, and usually when I do, I attract a sizable crowd.

EILEEN. *(playfully)* Yeah, well freakshows usually do.

AL. *(smiling)* Oh, that's not right! You went over the line there – you took it too far!

*(**EILEEN** touches his hand.)*

EILEEN. I'm just kidding. I promise when you sunbathe in the nude, I'll call all the local tabloids and let them know you're out there.

AL. Nah, see, the whole reason I wanna take this place is so I can get *away* from the tabloids.

EILEEN. Oh, *I* see.

AL. Well no you don't, 'cause quite frankly you don't know what it's like being in the spotlight all the time, hounded by obsessive fans – mostly women, ravenous for my company – but I appreciate your sympathy, however misguided it is.

EILEEN. What'd you memorize that? That was the longest sentence I ever heard.

(**AL** *chuckles, picks up the bottle and starts to pour* **EILEEN** *some wine.*)

(*stopping him*) Oh no, that's okay.

AL. Nah, come on, have a little – I'm buying.

(**EILEEN** *pulls her glass away.*)

EILEEN. No really – stop.

(**AL** *suddenly realizes his mistake.*)

AL. Aw shit, I totally forgot. The uh, the *program*.

EILEEN. Yes, the program.

AL. No, I totally forgot, I swear.

EILEEN. No, it's okay. (*She clears her throat.*) So. I take it you want to make an offer then.

AL. Oh yeah I mean uh...so wait a minute, you can't even have a glass?

EILEEN. Uh, no.

AL. But I mean what's *one* glass really gonna do, y'know?

EILEEN. Well, it would make me want to have *another* glass, and then *another* glass, and so on and so forth until I either passed out or started dancing on that table over there.

AL. Well, these tables are pretty small, I don't know if they could handle your weight.

EILEEN. Oh, thanks a lot!

AL. Oh no, I didn't mean that! I just meant these tables are tiny, y'know. I feel like I'm right on top of you.

(**AL** *awkwardly tries to scoot backwards. He's still very close to* **EILEEN**.)

EILEEN. Yup, they really pack 'em in here at Valencia. Part of the charm.

AL. Yeah, I never been here before. Fancy. *(beat)* So what about one *sip?*

EILEEN. Uh – again: it would lead to another sip, then another, and –

AL. And so on and so forth, till you're dancing on the table.

EILEEN. Exactly. It all ends the same way – with me dancing on the table. *(beat)* Anyway, I assume you want to make an offer on the house, right?

AL. And then everyone else has to get drunk, just so they're able to bear the sight of you dancing.

EILEEN. Uh, yes exactly.

AL. So really, you not drinking is a very *altruistic* gesture.

EILEEN. *(smiling)* What'd you, read the dictionary recently?

AL. Yeah, I've been brushing up on my dictionary.

EILEEN. Well, you know what? It is *altruistic* of me. 'Cause I was a real drag to be around when I was drunk. I mean you think I'm mean now, you should've seen me back in the day.

AL. Back in the day? You're young – I mean how long you been sober for?

EILEEN. I've been in recovery for, oh, a little over two years now.

AL. So how does that work anyway – "recovery" or whatever?

EILEEN. How does it work?

AL. Yeah, I mean those meetings. What do you say aside from, "Hey my name is Al, so on and so forth."

EILEEN. Well –

AL. I mean you, what – you tell stories about your life and what not?

EILEEN. Yeah, y'know –

AL. And I mean, you make new friends obviously. But does it really change you?

EILEEN. *(gently)* Well, if you let me finish, I promise I'll tell you.

AL. Sorry, sorry. I'm just interested for some reason, I don't know why.

(He's nervous to be so close to her.)

EILEEN. I can see that. Basically, yeah, you tell stories. I mean it's not easy cause you're fighting your own urges all day long, y'know? And that constant fighting just, um, further amplifies the pain you feel over and over again throughout the day.

AL. The pain? The pain of what?

EILEEN. *(a little self-conscious)* I don't know. The pain of… monotonous living I guess? Um.

*(**AL** is now completely in love.)*

AL. Uh, so did you like *(He clears his throat.)* did like something happen? Specifically I mean.

EILEEN. *(chuckling self-consciously)* You mean was there a specific incident that made me hit bottom and try to 'fight my way back up'? Um, yeah, actually, sort of.

AL. What was it.

EILEEN. I, um, *(She laughs at herself.)* God, this is so stupid.

AL. No, no. Keep going.

EILEEN. I basically – I uh, *(She takes a deep breath.)* I woke my mom's cat up from a nap.

*(**AL** waits for the rest. It doesn't come.)*

AL. What, that's it?

EILEEN. Well it just…it started this whole chain reaction, y'know? I mean basically what happened is, two years ago, right before I got sober, I went home for Thanksgiving. And the night I arrived, first thing I did is I went straight to the local bar and started drinking *really* heavily. I mean, one – it was my birthday, cause my birthday was on Thanksgiving that year, and I was *really* depressed. And two – it was ladies night, buy one get one free – so that right there just, like, doubled the incentive to get wasted. So I just drank and drank til it got to the point where you close your eyes and it feels like you're on a really wobbly carousel? Anyway, I woke up the next morning, and I had to pee *so* badly. And I didn't think I was gonna make it to the bathroom at the end of the hall. So instead, I just went into my mom's room next door and used her bathroom. But when I got out, I saw the cat was taking a nap on my mom's bed – and he looked so *cute* y'know? – so naturally, I just started petting it. But apparently he didn't *want* me to pet him – because what he did is he got up and he ran away from me – he ran downstairs where the *other* place he liked to sleep was, right behind the kitchen sink. But downstairs my mom was cooking, making this special dish or something, and she had my grandmother's priceless antique bowl out, and when my cat jumped up onto the kitchen counter to get to his *other* resting place, he of course knocked over my grandmother's priceless antique bowl, causing it to shatter everywhere, which in turn caused my mom to start yelling and cursing and crying about how her mom's priceless antique bowl was now gone forever, because the cat had destroyed it. But don't you see? *I'm* the one who destroyed it – *I* broke the bowl! Cause if I hadn't've drank so much the night before, I wouldn't've had to pee so badly, I wouldn't've had to use my mom's bathroom, I wouldn't've seen the cat sleeping there, gone to pet him, et cetera, et cetera – the bowl would still be intact! But that's when I realized that *this* is the way the world works, y'know? You, you sneeze and a person dies. You leave your book on the bus, and a war breaks out! I mean if one thing leads to another, how can you *do* anything? How can you get up in the morning, say hi to someone, eat a meal? I move my hand this way and somewhere a kid starts crying! So *of course* life is monotonous! I mean we have no choice but to be as monotonous as possible!

Because if we're not – if I keep drinking and peeing without thinking of anyone else – sooner or later the whole world gets destroyed! *(She leans forward.)* And I mean doesn't that scare the living shit out of you?

(AL lunges forward and kisses her. She pushes him away.)

EILEEN. *(cont.)* What are you doing?

AL. Holy shit, I don't know. I'm sorry, just watching you, I got sucked in, I don't know!

(He starts breathing heavily.)

EILEEN. Okay, calm down, Al.

AL. Shit, I don't know what happened. I'm sorry, I shouldn't have done that!

(He's trembling. She takes his hand and steadies him.)

EILEEN. No it's okay. You just, you startled me is all. It's okay.

AL. Is it okay?

EILEEN. *(nodding)* It's okay.

(He lunges in and kisses her again. She pushes him away.)

Well, don't do it again!

AL. What, you *just* said "it's okay!"

EILEEN. Yeah, "it's okay" as in I'm not gonna press charges! Not as in "do it again"!

AL. Well…well fuck! I thought you meant, y'know – like yeah I caught you by surprise *that* time, but really, y'know…you wanted to kiss me.

EILEEN. Well then let me make it clear: I Don't Want To Kiss You, Al.

(AL looks away hurt.)

Jesus, I'm sorry – that came out wrong.

AL. No, it's fine. That's all you had to say. You shoulda said that the first time.

EILEEN. I know Al, I'm just…I'm really sorry.

AL. What are *you* sorry for? I'm the one who fucked things up. I gotta go to the bathroom.

(AL gets up. EILEEN looks down. As AL walks to the bathroom, DANIEL walks in from the other room, already a bit drunk, holding a camera. He purposefully bumps into AL as AL walks by.)

(not looking up) Sorry.

(AL continues to the bathroom. DANIEL makes an 'up yours' signal to AL's back, then resumes his path to EILEEN's table. He sits down in AL's seat, startling her.)

EILEEN. Daniel?!

DANIEL. *(triumphantly)* You fucked up.

(DANIEL leans back victoriously, causing his chair to fall over. He quickly gets up, puts the chair back, and sits down again.)

You *fucked* up! And at Valencia of all places – our old stomping grounds!

EILEEN. What the hell are you doing here?

DANIEL. I followed you, you idiot. I thought for sure you spotted me at the Gersten's Open House.

EILEEN. Okay – this has to stop.

DANIEL. I'll tell you what has to stop – your reign of power. You're finished. *(He holds up the camera.)* Because right here, I got all the proof I need! I knew following you would pay off and *man* it did. Y'know, the ironic thing is that I actually believed he was just a client of yours for most of the day!

EILEEN. He *is* just a client – it's not what it looks like. And even it was, so what?! We're separated!

DANIEL. Well, let's see how our lawyers spin it – let's see if Goldberg can you get you out of this one. 'Cause here's a list for you, Lister: one – this picture, along with all the other ones I took today, does not bode well for you. And two – the reason why has nothing to do with hook-up sessions before and/or after our separation.

EILEEN. What the hell are you talking about?

DANIEL. Try this on for size: Al Gurvis...is a non-resident alien in this country.

EILEEN. A what? You're full of shit.

DANIEL. Oh really? Go ahead and ask him. Better yet ask yourself: why were you trying to give a non-resident alien a place of permanent residency? Because according to U.S. Immigration Law – *that*'s illegal. And even Goldberg can't get you out of that one. Then ask yourself, "Do I really want Goldberg representing me? *Maybe*, I want to settle this little divorce affair out of court – and give my ex-husband pretty much everything he asks for – or else *maybe* he'll get my realtor's license taken away, and even send me to jail."

EILEEN. You're blackmailing me?!

DANIEL. You blue-balled me!

EILEEN. You're a disgusting animal!

DANIEL. That may be. But you ask yourself those questions. And in the meantime, I'll ask *myself* if I can ever get over seeing the former love of my life, making out with some two-bit hoodlum, at our favorite restaurant.

(**DANIEL** *exits.* **EILEEN** *doesn't know what to do. She looks at the glass of wine, tempted for a moment.* **AL** *re-enters and sits back down, recovered somewhat from before.*)

AL. All right, look – I know I fucked up. But let's just move on. Truth is, I'm just really lucky to have met you and, honest to God, I can't thank you enough for all you've done for me. I mean Jesus – one fucking weekend, and suddenly I feel like I can turn things around in my life. So yes, I apologize, and yes, I'd like to make an offer on the house.

EILEEN. Are you a non-resident alien.

AL. What? Who the fuck told you that?

EILEEN. Is it true.

AL. I mean...I don't know, sort of. But if I get this house, I'll be a resident.

EILEEN. Jesus Christ, Al – that's not how it works!

AL. Well I don't know how it works, you tell me.

EILEEN. Well first you get what we call in this country a Green Card.

AL. Yeah, I know – I'm working on it. You don't have to patronize me.

EILEEN. You could've cost me my license! You still might!

AL. Okay, well I'm sorry! I mean there's other things more important in this world than licenses, right? Like helping a guy out.

EILEEN. "Helping a guy out?" What – you mean like sleeping with him?

AL. Aw, fuck you.

EILEEN. Fuck you! You took advantage of me!

(**EILEEN** *gets up.* **AL** *gets up after her.*)

AL. Wait, I didn't mean to, okay?! I just thought I could buy a place of my own is all! If you're saying I'm not allowed to do that or whatever, okay, then – I didn't know that! I mean I could never even afford one 'til now – 'til you came and helped me out! But I thought it was like *fate* or whatever that brought us together, y'know?

(*She walks right up to him.*)

EILEEN. It's *not* fate Al. There's no such thing as *fate*, so grow up! (*She sighs.*) It's all just dumb luck. Just dumb luck, Al.

(**EILEEN** *exits.* **AL** *just stares ahead, crushed.*)

End of Scene

Scene Seven

*(Monday morning. Film set. **BARRY** stands by the craft
service table, munching loudly on a bag of chips. A big
box of chocolates sits on the table. **AL** walks in and goes
straight for the coffee.)*

AL. *(without looking up)* Hey.

BARRY. What up, Allie. You see the game yesterday?

AL. No.

BARRY. Get this: Mets blew a four-two lead, lost their sixth
straight. Reyes got his 60th though. That fucker can
run, huh?

AL. Yup.

> *(**AL** takes a stirrer and stirs his coffee. He stops when he
> sees the big box on the table.)*

What's this.

BARRY. What, that box right there that says 'Ghiradelli
Chocolates?' Beats the shit out of me.

> *(**BARRY** hits **AL** playfully on the arm.)*

Nah, it's a little gift. Don't worry about it.

> *(**BARRY** goes back to munching chips. **AL** looks down at
> the box.)*

AL. *(still looking down)* I didn't win, so…

BARRY. Huh?

AL. *(louder)* I said I didn't win the bet! In fact, I lost, okay?!

BARRY. Jesus, lower your voice, Al.

AL. No, I lost the fucking bet! Is that what you want to
hear?! What you want me to say! That I was wrong?!
That you were right and the world really *is* a completely and totally fucked up place, huh? HUH?!

> *(**AL** starts to tear up.)*

Is that what you want! Fine, so I'll say it okay? You
were right, Barry, and I was wrong! Thanks to people
like you – *assholes* like you, who don't give a shit about

anyone but themselves – people like me get fucked! Okay? I got *fucked*! And I was wrong to think I wouldn't get fucked in this world, okay?! I was wrong and I got fucked! So here, eat your fucking chips!

(**AL** *starts throwing the various bags from the craft service table at* **BARRY**.)

BARRY. Hey c'mon! Cut it out!

AL. Eat 'em up! Eat 'em all up! Keep stuffing your fucking face and living your meaningless life while I sit here getting fucked! Getting fucked by all this shit!

(**AL** *flips the entire craft service table, toppling over everything on it.*)

BARRY. Jesus Christ, Al, get a hold of yourself!

(**AL** *stands there breathing heavily.*)

AL. I tried, okay. I tried my goddamn hardest…and I failed. Is that what you want to hear? That I failed? Well I did! *I. Failed!*

(*He picks up the Ghiradelli Chocolates box.*)

So here – you take your stupid chocolates! You take 'em…and you shove 'em!

(**AL** *rips the box open. Hundreds of business cards pour out from the box and line the floor.* **AL** *stops when he sees them. He slowly picks one up and looks at it.*)

(*genuinely stunned*) What are these? These aren't chocolates.

BARRY. No they're not…you maniac. They're business cards. I stopped by the printers last Friday after work and saw that that drunk chick Eileen Lee had returned your cards. 'Cept they had typos all over them. So I ordered you some new ones.

AL. (*reading*) "Al Gurvis – Professional Gaffing Assistant… slash Electrician."

BARRY. You said you wanted some business cards, so I got you some fucking business cards.

(AL *looks at* **BARRY**, *extremely touched. He tries not to cry. He nods.*)

AL. Thank you.

(**BARRY** *is extremely uncomfortable with* **AL**'*s display of emotion.*)

BARRY. Y'know. No biggie. I didn't think you'd flip out over it.

(**AL** *gets down on the ground and begins to pick everything up. After a moment,* **BARRY** *comes and helps him.*)

AL. Everyone's watching me.

BARRY. Yeah no shit – you went nutso.

(*They pick everything up.* **BARRY** *looks at* **AL** *who has his head down.*)

(*after a moment*) So was she Asian?

(**AL** *chuckles and shakes his head, no.*)

Well, you can't win 'em all, am I right?

(**AL** *nods and sniffles.* **BARRY** *picks up the craft service table.*)

Hey you still got cable at your place?

(**AL** *nods and sniffles.*)

All right, I'm coming over tonight to watch the game. Even *they* can't lose another one, right? It's sheer odds. Even The Mets gotta get lucky once. (*beat*) Hey Al – we been friends for what, five, six years now?

AL. Yeah, something like that.

BARRY. So how come you never told me you were into old muscle cars? I fucking *love* old muscle cars.

(**AL** *looks at him, confused. Lights out.*)

End of Play

ABOUT THE PLAYWRIGHT

Josh Koenigsberg's play *Al's Business Cards* was a *New York Times* "Critic's Pick" during its run at the Lion Theater in New York City in 2009. He won the 2010 Samuel French Off Off Broadway festival for his short play *Dance Lessons*. His work has been developed at The Public Theater, Atlantic Theater Company, Second Stage, Naked Angels, Ars Nova, The Old Vic, among others. He is a founding ensemble member of At Play, as well as a member of the Old Vic New Voices Network, the Ars Nova Playgroup and The Dramatist's Guild. He is currently one of the staff writers for the podcast "Naked Radio."

Josh has written several screenplays with Simon Rich, the most recent being *Seymour Escapes From Alcatraz!* He has an M.F.A. in playwriting from Columbia University and a B.A. in Philosophy and the Arts from Bard College.

OTHER TITLES AVAILABLE FROM SAMUEL FRENCH

OFF OFF BROADWAY FESTIVAL PLAYS, 35TH SERIES

Various Authors

One of Manhattan's most established play festivals, the Samuel French Off Off Broadway Short Play Festival fosters the work of emerging writers, giving them the exposure of publication and representation.

The festival resulting in this collection was held July 13th-18th, 2010 at Theatre Row on 42nd Street in New York City.

From the initial pool of over 850 submissions, the Final Forty plays were chosen to be performed over a period of one week. A panel of judges comprised of celebrity playwrights, theatrical agents and artistic directors nominated one or more of each evening's plays as finalists. The final round was then held on the last day of the festival. Out of these plays, six winners listed below were chosen by Samuel French, Inc. to receive publication and licensing contracts.

Winning plays and playwrights for this collection include:

Skin Deep by Mary Lynn Dobson
The Pigskin by Gabriel Jason Dean
White Embers by Saviana Stanescu
The Bear (A Tragedy) by EJC Calvert
Dance Lessons by Josh Koenigsberg
The Mud is Thicker in Mississippi by Dennis A. Allen II